The JOKE Book

for people who think DONALD TRUMP is a joke

by THE UNKNOWN COMIC

BearManor Media
Albany, Georgia

The Joke Book for People Who Think Donald Trump is a Joke
© 2013 The Unknown Comic. All rights reserved.

No part of this book may be reproduced in any form or by any means, electronic, mechanical, digital, photocopying or recording, except for the inclusion in a review, without permission in writing from the publisher.

Published in the USA by:
BearManor Media
PO Box 1129
Duncan, OK 73534-1129
www.BearManorMedia.com

ISBN-10: 1593932588
ISBN-13: 1-59393-258-8

Cover design and layout by Allan T. Duffin.

Printed in the United States of America

The JOKE Book

for people who think DONALD TRUMP is a joke

Before compiling this collection of Trump Jokes, I have to admit, I did read Donald Trump's book, *How to Get Rich*, cover to cover and found it interesting... not the pages... just the covers.

The Beginning

On September 10, 1945, witnesses claim a Spaceship with Five Aliens aboard crashed on a Mule and Donkey ranch 50 miles outside New York City—an incident they say has been covered up by the military. On June 14, 1946—almost exactly Nine Months after that day—Donald Trump was born. That clears up a lot of things.

The Unknown Comic

Whenever I go swimming in the Ocean, I always wear a T-Shirt that reads... "Donald Trump would make a Great President"... because I figure Even a Shark wouldn't Swallow that.

—

In the U.S.A. all Men are born Free and Equal... except for Donald Trump,
who was born a little more free and equal...

—

The saddest moment for a child is not when he learns that Santa Claus isn't real. It's when he learns that Donald Trump is.

Blue-collar workers like Basketball.
White-collar workers like Tennis.
Heads of companies such as Donald Trump like Golf.
Which means, the more successful you become...
The smaller your balls get.

on Donald Trump

Donald Trump is a Man of Few Words, unless they're about him.

Donald Trump is outspoken... but not by many...

Donald Trump is truly HIS own best friend...

Donald Trump believes HE is not conceited, though he admits HE has every right to be...

Donald Trump believes that everything is for the best... and that HE is the best...

Donald Trump always knows when an idea is terrific... when it's HIS...

Donald Trump believes in Free Speech... except when it's about HIM...

Donald Trump believes the less you have... the more there is for him to get...

Donald Trump is never too busy to stop and talk about how busy HE is.

Donald Trump is the smartest man in the world. And that's not just my opinion, it's HIS.

Donald Trump is now married but there are rumors he will go back to his
First Love... Himself.

Donald Trump can do without everything in this world... except self-indulgence.

Donald Trump always thinks twice before saying nothing.

Donald Trump is a man who thinks HE knows more than you do... and doesn't hide it.

Donald Trump thinks that all the world is a "Stooge."

Donald Trump will stand for what HE thinks others will fall for.

Donald Trump thinks HE'S a great LOVER, because HE always finishes first.

Donald Trump believes Golf is great exercise... especially climbing in and out of that Cart.

Donald Trump is always Me-Deep in conversation.

Donald Trump would like to have HIS Cake... and yours too.

Donald Trump is One Person who can say absolutely Nothing... and mean it.

Donald Trump believes HE is too good to be true.

Donald Trump has what it takes... to take what you've got.

Donald Trump doesn't care which side HIS bread is buttered on...
because HE eats both sides anyway.

Too often, Donald Trump has nothing to say, but that doesn't stop him from saying it...

There's something to be said about Donald Trump... and HE'S usually saying it.

One good thing about Donald Trump is HE doesn't talk about anyone else.

If they ever think of putting Donald Trump's head on Mount Rushmore, it would be easy... "It's the right size."

If Donald Trump had to live his life all over again... He'd still fall in love with himself all over again.

Donald Trump is a true Optimist... because HE doesn't care what happens...
as long as it happens to someone else...

Donald Trump is a man of Untold Wealth... because HE doesn't report most of it on his Income Tax return.

When all is said and done... Donald Trump will keep on talking...

The only thing Donald Trump has that gets bigger when you stroke it...
is his EGO.

Some Men are born Great... Some Men achieve Greatness... Donald Trump thrust greatness upon himself.

on FAME

Some people think Donald Trump's head is getting too BIG and that he combs his hair over to hide the "stretch marks."

Donald Trump actually believes that if he wasn't born... people would wonder why.

Donald Trump believes that his Doctor is jealous of his fame. Last year for his birthday, he sent Trump a carton of cigarettes...

Donald Trump never forgot how his older sister used to help clean up after him when he was a kid... so when he became successful and began making lots of money... he hired her as a maid.

—

on
PHILOSOPHY

Donald Trump believes... "Life is like a Shit Sandwich... the more Bread you have... the less Shit you have to eat..."

Donald Trump believes... that whether you're rich or poor... it's nice to have money...

Donald Trump believes... the only thing worse than people talking about you behind your back... is people Not talking about you behind your back.

Donald Trump believes it's better to give than to receive... as long as it's Tax Deductible.

Donald Trump believes Most women are really interested in a man's company...
if he owns it.

Donald Trump believes that Money can't buy happiness... but it's still more comfortable crying in a Mercedes than on a bicycle.

Donald Trump believes that You can't fool all the people all the time... but he's content with a sizable majority.

Donald Trump believes it's better to know you know, than just to know.

Donald Trump believes a man with 10 Billion Dollars... is No Happier than a Man with 9 Billion dollars.

Donald Trump believes that a man with 10 million dollars is happier that a man with 10 kids... because a man with 10 million dollars wants more.

Donald Trump believes that before you criticize someone, you should walk a mile in their shoes. That way, after you criticize them, you're a mile away... and you've got their shoes.

on POLITICS

Donald Trump for President? Politicians are Public Servants... Does anyone really believe Donald Trump could be anyone's Servant?

Donald Trump says to his wife, "I'm thinking of going into Politics." His wife says, "Honestly?" Trump replies, "Well, I don't know about that..."

Donald Trump is qualified to be in Politics because he doesn't drink, smoke or do drugs... In fact, his only vice is lying...

When Donald Trump talks Politics, you know he comes from the wrong side of the facts.

Donald Trump is convinced the economy would be in better shape if the poor would just spend more money.

Donald Trump believes that We're not in a recession... We're just experiencing the worst "Boom" in history.

Donald Trump... a man who is willing to lay down your life... for his country.

Donald Trump believes that the United States is the greatest country in the world... because he was born in it.

Donald Trump loves his country and wants to make as much out of it as possible.

When it comes to Politics, Donald Trump is like a Fog Horn... He repeatedly calls attention to the problem... but never does anything about it.

Donald Trump believes that today... an honest Politician is one who, when he is bought... stays bought...

Donald Trump believes in Capital Punishment... as long as it's not too severe...

on WEALTH

For some people, life isn't so bad. Or as Donald Trump might say, "Another day, another 425,000 dollars."

Donald Trump Makes lots of Money...... most of the rest of us have to Earn Money...

Donald Trump believes people should feel sorry for him because he's never had that thrill you get when you make your last payment on something.

Donald Trump once woke up terrified after having a nightmare... He dreamt he was only worth $50 million.

Donald Trump thinks there are two classes of people... The have-Nots...
and the Have-Yachts.

Donald Trump worships the ground he walks on... because there's a good chance he owns it.

Donald Trump believes that Happiness can't buy Money.

Donald Trump believes that Money isn't everything... sometimes it's barely 99%.

Donald Trump believes that the Five Secrets to Happiness are... Money, Money, Money, Money and Money.

Donald Trump believes that money can't buy happiness... but it can make you very comfortable while you're unhappy.

Donald Trump believes that there's more to life than Money. There's also credit cards, stocks, bonds, gold, jewelry and diamonds.

Donald Trump believes that there are more important things in life than Money... but they won't go out with you if you don't have any.

Donald Trump believes there are Five ways to become a Millionaire...
Inherit it - Earn it - Marry it - win the lottery - or Sue.

Donald Trump believes that Money is "Not" the Key to Happiness... but if you have enough of it... you can get a Key made.

Donald Trump believes that today, the only thing you get for a dollar...
are quarters, dimes, nickels and pennies.

on SUCCESS

Donald Trump believes that if at first you don't succeed... you're 99% of the population...

Donald Trump believes HE is successful... because he didn't have the advantages others had...

Donald Trump believes a College education is very necessary in Business... especially at Office Parties when someone is needed to mix the Cocktails.

Donald Trump believes if at first you don't succeed... try again when nobody is watching.

Donald Trump believes if at first you don't succeed... you're probably not related to the Boss.

Donald Trump believes, "Why climb the Ladder of Success... if an elevator is available?"

Donald Trump's 8 rules for Success

Never invest your money in anything that "Eats."

Never underestimate the power of Stupid People... in large groups.

Never bet on a Sure Thing, unless you can afford to lose.

Never call anyone Stupid, until you first find out if they'll lend you Fifty Bucks.

Never cross a Bridge... before it's been built.

Never interrupt someone... who is flattering you.

Never start a business... in a Fireproof Building.

Never stop to think... you might forget to start again.

Donald Trump's Advice for Success

The best way to save money... is to not spend it...

If your neighbors need Food... Give them Food... If they need Water... Give them Water... If they need Money... Give them Water...

Put most of your money under your mattress... That way, you'll always have something to fall back on...

Don't believe in the phrase..."Tomorrow is the first day of the rest of your life"... because nobody likes to hire beginners...

Put some of your money in Taxes... it's the only sure thing to go up...

Learn a trade... That way you will always know what kind of work you're out of...

Always stay nice to people... until you become a millionaire... then they'll be nice to you...

Forgive your enemy... but remember the bastard's name.

How Rich is Donald Trump?

Last Christmas he was in Europe, where he bought a Picasso, a Rembrandt and a Van Gogh.... He then said, "Okay, we got the cards. Now let's go find some presents."

Donald Trump actually paid to have his pregnant wife's morning sickness... changed to the afternoon.

As a kid Donald Trump owned a Rolls Royce bicycle.

Donald Trump has an air-conditioned Sauna.

Donald Trump's bathrooms all have Gold Toilet Seats.... Trump says, "They're expensive... but what a way to go."

When Donald Trump was in college... he would hire someone to write home
for money for him.

(actual Donald Trump quotes)

"I have a great relationship with the Blacks..."

"The beauty of me is that I'm very Rich..."

Donald Trump mis-QUOTES

"When I was a kid in school, everybody hated me because I was so popular."

"Admit Your Faults.... I would, if I had any."

"Charisma is that indescribable something... that Billionaires have."

"It's lonely at the top... but you eat better."

"I feel sorry for school Kids today.... If they don't learn to write their own name... when they grow up, they'll have to pay Cash for Everything."

Little-known facts about Donald Trump

Contrary to popular belief... Donald Trump was NOT born in a "Manger"...

Donald Trump was born with a silver spoon up his ass.

Donald Trump's bath towels read... His and His.

Donald Trump is not a stubborn man... He'll agree with anyone who thinks
HE'S brilliant...

As a kid, Donald Trump collected from the Tooth Fairy over 100 times before
he was 10.

As a kid, when Donald Trump played Doctor, One would operate and the other would sue.

Donald Trump was once so depressed that he tried to commit suicide by having his Chauffeur drive him over a cliff.

When Donald Trump has an orgasm… he screams out his own name.

Every year on his Birthday, Donald Trump sends his parents a card of congratulations.

Donald Trump used to be an atheist… until he found out he was God.

Donald Trump once had to pay an emergency visit to his psychiatrist when he started thinking that other people were just as good as he.

Every Sunday Donald Trump always flips a coin to see if HE'S going to go to church or go play golf… One Sunday, HE had to flip that coin 14 times…

Donald Trump plans on being buried in one of his Golf Courses... which would make him an "Ass-hole in One."

Donald Trump once invested in a Halfway House... for girls who don't go all the way...

Donald Trump's kids are not spoiled... they always smell that way...

Donald Trump once donated his sperm to the Harvard Medical Center and later wrote it off on his taxes as sending his kids to college.

Next year, Donald Trump will introduce a new aftershave lotion he believes will attract women... it smells like money...

Things you'll never see

Donald Trump meeting someone he thinks is as smart as he is.

—

The difference between a Frenchman and Donald Trump is... When a Frenchman walks into a restaurant, he acts as if he owns it.... When Donald Trump walks into a restaurant, he acts as if he doesn't give a shit who owns it....

More Trump Jokes

Donald Trump told his wife that one of these days he's going to pass on and asked her to find a nice burial place for him. Two weeks later, she said, "I found a perfect spot on a hill overlooking a beautiful stream. The Sun hits it during the day almost as if you were being spotlighted." "Sounds good." Trump asked, "How much is it?" "100,000 dollars," his wife replied. "100,000 dollars?" shouted Trump. "But I'm only going to be there 3 days!"...

Donald Trump says to his wife, "If I were disfigured would you still love me?"
She replies, "Yes, I'll always love you." Trump asks, "What if I got sick and couldn't make love any more. Would you still love me?" She replies, "Don't worry, darling. I'll always love you." Trump again asks, "What if I lost all my money and became poor. Would you still love me then?" His wife replies, "Donald, yes I'd still love you, but most of all, I'd really miss you."

Donald Trump, visiting London on a business trip, is led into a hotel room by a bellhop and sees a gorgeous Woman Naked on his Bed. Trump yells at the bellhop, "What the hell is the meaning of this? Are you trying to cause a scandal? I'm a married man and you try to offend me like this. I'm going to sue this Hotel." As he continues the woman begins dressing and slides from the bed. Trump quickly turns to her and says, "Where are you going? No one's talking to you!"

Donald Trump and the Mayor of New York city are playing Golf together. They come to a stop because the golfers ahead of them are playing very slowly. Angry, Donald Trump says, "What's with them? Can't they hurry?" The Mayor says, "This is ridiculous." He sees a worker on the side and asks, "What's their problem?" The Worker explains, "They're Blind firefighters who lost their sight saving the clubhouse from a fire, so they can play for free anytime." The Mayor says, "How sad. I'll donate money to their union." Donald Trump says, "Why the fuck can't they play at NIGHT?"

Donald Trump dies. The Devil tells him they have a special section for celebrities and offers him 3 ways to spend eternity: First, the Devil shows him Wilt Chamberlain chained with several women whipping him. Trump says, "That's not good. What else you got?" The Devil then shows him George Carlin, who is being forced to listen to Rush Limbaugh for eternity. Trump says, "I love Limbaugh, but that's not for me, either." So the Devil shows him his final option, where Richard Nixon is tied up and Anna Nicole Smith is giving him Oral Sex. Trumps eyes light up and he says, "This I'll take!" The Devil says, "OK," then yells out, "Hey Anna... you've been replaced."

Donald Trump dies and is stopped at the Pearly Gates by St. Peter, who says, "Sorry, but we don't allow the SUPER RICH into Heaven anymore." "What?" replies Trump. "Why not?" "Well, we just don't." Trump complains until St. Peter says, "Well, have you ever done any good for those less fortunate than you?" Trump says, "Yeah. Just the other day a lady stopped me on the street collecting for a children's charity and I gave her 10 dollars. Last week I donated 10 dollars to the Cancer Society, and today a homeless guy asked me for money and I gave him 10 dollars." "Alright," says St. Peter, "let me go talk to God." Five minutes later St. Peter returns and says to Trump: "I've spoken with God and he agrees with me. Here's your 30 bucks back. Now fuck off!"

Donald Trump is driving in his car when he sees a man eating grass. Trump stops and says to the man, "Why are you eating grass?" The Man sadly replies, "I have no money for food and I am so hungry." Trump says, "Listen, hop in my car. I'm taking you to my house." "But I'm with my wife and two children." He points behind a tree. "They are also eating grass." "Bring them with you," Trump replies. So they all get in the car and as Trump drives off, the man says, "Thank you so much for taking us with you." Trump replies, "No problem. You're going to love my place. The grass is over two feet high."

—

Actual Celebrity Quotes

"The good news is, President Obama was born in America. The bad news is, so was Donald Trump."
—Jay Leno

"The only time Donald Trump scares me is when I don't see him on TV in over a week. I like knowing where he is!"
—Gary Shandling

"Donald Trump announced he got his own segment every Monday morning on Fox News. Just what Fox News needs—another blonde airhead."
—Bill Maher

"This is what I've been waiting for my whole life. A President who's not afraid to tell the truth about being a lying asshole."
—Lewis Black

"They have to put Trump on every program, spewing his crazy ideas, because his poll numbers are so high. And his poll numbers are so high because they put him on every program, spewing his crazy ideas."
—Jon Stewart

"I'm interested in seeing the long form of Donald Trump's death certificate."
—Joel West

"Donald Trump is a Pompous Asshole! Saw him in Aspen with one D-cup chick after another. Everyone up there thought he was a complete idiot."
—Cher

"Trump water. Blah! Trump Magazine. Blah! Trump steaks. Blah! Trump vodka. Blah! When you're so desperate to make a dollar you have to put your name [on] everything, and then you have to comment on everything."
—Mark Cuban

"I don't think he has that much credibility. I don't understand why people pay any attention to him."
—Ron Paul

The Unknown Comic

"Donald Trump is a "Bloviating ignoramus" and redundant evidence that if your net worth is high enough, your IQ can be very low and you can still intrude into American politics."
—George Will

"Donald Trump is like a snake-oil salesman.... "He returns—like a raging herpes rash... He wants me... He needs me—he's obsessed... like a grandpa stalker."
—Rosie O'Donnell

"That poor pathetic man."
—Barbara Walters

"He's full of it... You run or shut up... Well, the only thing he's running is his mouth."
—Bill Cosby

"You don't want to engage with somebody that's so grotesque."
—Zach Galifianakis

"The world does not revolve around his penis."
—Gloria Allred

"I love Donald Trump, all comedians love Donald Trump. If God gave comedians the power to invent people, the first person we would invent is Donald Trump... God's gift to comedy."
—Jerry Seinfeld

"The previous lines are not insults... they are observations..."
 —the unknown comic

Celebrity Quotes about Donald Trump's Hair

"If Trump does become president, I hope he puts a wig on his plane and calls it Hair Force One."
—Jimmy Kimmel

"Donald Trump has a great campaign slogan: 'A complex world demands complex hair.'"
—David Letterman

"Donald Trump showed his birth certificate to reporters. Who cares about his birth certificate? I want to know if that thing on his head has had its vaccinations."
—Craig Ferguson

"Donald Trump often appears on Fox, which is ironic because a fox often appears on Donald Trump's head.
—Seth Meyers

"Donald Trump might be running for president and he just released his birth certificate. It lists his eyes as 'blue' and his hair as 'ridiculous.'"
—Conan O'Brien

"He wants to see Obama's birth certificate, I want to see his hairline. I think that's actually a helmet!"
—Robin Williams

Donald Trump said he still wants to look more closely at Obama's birth certificate to make sure that it's real. Incidentally, President Obama said the same exact thing about Donald Trump's hair."
—Jimmy Fallon

Donald Trump's head is getting too big for his toupee.
—The Unknown Comic

End Notes

I don't know what gave Donald Trump such a huge ego... but whatever it was... it worked.

Donald Trump would be Broke if he had to pay Taxes on what he thinks
he's worth.

Donald Trump reportedly spent over a million dollars on his gravesite...
Boy, those Rich People sure know how to Live.

Donald Trump will go down in the Anals of history... or is it Annals?
No... it's Anals.

Donald Trump will one day find out that He who dies with the most toys...
still dies...

Donald Trump will one day discover that Cemeteries are full of people who thought the world couldn't get along without them.

Thank you Donald Trump

... And a Few More...

Donald Trump is so Rich he could retire off the interest of his interests...

Donald Trump is so Rich, he once got a boy for his dog...

Donald Trump is so Rich, he has solid gold silverware..

The Unknown Comic

Donald Trump is so Rich, he refuses to be in the same car with his Chauffeur.

Donald Trump is so Rich, he has Swiss Money in American Banks...

Donald Trump is so Rich, he once cashed a check... and the Bank bounced...

Donald Trump is so Rich... he has no idea whose Picture is on the One Dollar Bill.

Donald Trump is so Rich, when he was a Teenager... he used to take his dates to a Drive in Movie in a Taxi...

Donald Trump is so Rich... he has a Green Thumb... from counting his money...

Donald Trump is so Rich... his suits cost $100 dollars to clean.

Donald Trump doesn't wash his hands... He has them dry cleaned.

Donald Trump has little diamonds in the rings under his eyes.

Donald Trump wasn't always RICH
Donald Trump was once so poor... At his beach house, he could only afford to hire one lifeguard for his swimming pool.

Donald Trump was once so poor... He had to build his penthouse
in the basement...

Donald Trump was once so poor... He had to raise his own Caviar...

Donald Trump was once so poor... His wife had to wear the previous years jewelry...

Donald Trump "Mis-Quote" Why should I put my money in banks..?...
I have more money than they do."

As a teen-ager, Donald Trump was once
spotted parked in Lovers lane
by himself.

As a teen-ager, Donald Trump would play
"Spin the bottle" by himself.

Success hasn't gone to Donald Trump's Head
as much as it's gone to his Mouth..

They say Exercise eliminates fat... So how
come Donald Trump has a double chin?

about the author

The Unknown Comic is a high school graduate who went to high school for 14 years, so he's no dummy. After high school, he went to one of the goodest colleges in the country where he majored in Bagology.

Originally from Bagdad, he left because having a bag over his head caused many of the men to think he was a woman. Tired of being a Sacks Symbol, he eventually escaped and ended up in SACKramento, California, where he moved in with his three cousins, Dirtbag, scumbag and douchebag.

The Unknown Comic decided to get into comedy when he realized people looked at him funny. Sadly, he recently looked up his family tree... and found out he was the Sap. That's why he hopes this book will sell in the hundreds and enable him to eventually buy a Gucci bag.

The Unknown Comic admits that he was half-bagged when writing most of this book. And Even though he now wears a Hefty Bag... he wants everyone to know that Sackcess has not gone to his head.

now,
flip this book

to read

The
Kardashian
Joke Book!

now,
flip this book

to read

The
Donald Trump
Joke Book!

and ended up in SACKramento, California, where he moved in with his three cousins, Dirtbag, scumbag and douchebag.

The Unknown Comic decided to get into comedy when he realized people looked at him funny. Sadly, he recently looked up his family tree... and found out he was the Sap. That's why he hopes this book will sell in the hundreds and enable him to eventually buy a Gucci bag.

The Unknown Comic admits that he was half-bagged when writing most of this book. And Even though he now wears a Hefty Bag... he wants everyone to know that Sackcess has not gone to his head.

about the author

The Unknown Comic is a high school graduate who went to high school for 14 years, so he's no dummy. After high school, he went to one of the goodest colleges in the country where he majored in Bagology.

Originally from Bagdad, he left because having a bag over his head caused many of the men to think he was a woman. Tired of being a Sacks Symbol, he eventually escaped

Kim kardashian and Kanye West are about to have sex for the first time. Kim is very excited and whispers, "Put a finger in." So he does. Getting more turned on Kim says, "Put another finger in." So he does. Now even more excited, she says, "Put your hand in." Kanye says, "My Hand?" "Yes", Kim replies, "Your hand! Put it in!" He does and now she's going crazy as she moans. "Put your other hand in." Kanye says, "My other hand?" "Yes. Please do it." She moans louder as Kanye slides his other hand in." She then cries out, "Now, Clap!" A surprised Kanye says, "I can't." Kim looks at him coyly and says, "Tight, huh?"

To the Kardashians.....

*Thank you
from The Unknown Comic...*

examine her. "You'll be fine," he said. Kim asked, "How long will it be before I am able to have a normal sex life again?" The Surgeon paused, which alarmed Kim. "What's the matter Doctor? I will be all right, won't I?" The Surgeon replied, "Yes, you'll be fine. It's just that no one has ever asked me that question after having their tonsils out."

Kim Kardashian is in bed with Kanye West. As they snuggle close to each other, Kanye asks Kim, "Honey, do you know how many others you've had sex with before me?" "Yes, of course I do," Kim replied. "So tell me, how many?" Kanye asked. Kim replied again, "Are you sure you want to know?" "Yes, I do," Kanye said, then asked again, "How many guys have you had sex with?" Kim responded, "All right, I'll tell you." There was silence as Kanye waited several minutes for an answer. Finally after several more minutes, Kanye said, "Well, I'm still waiting." And Kim replied, "Give me a few more minutes. I'm still counting."

good, I had twenty-five orgasms." Khloe says, "Wow... I didn't know your boyfriend is that good,. Kim replies, "Oh, you meant with only One guy..."

A businessman got on an elevator. When he entered, Kim Kardashian greeted him with a bright, "T-G-I-F." The man smiled at Kim and replied, "S-H-I-T." Kim looked puzzled and repeated, "T-G-I-F," more slowly. The man again answered, "S-H-I-T." Kim was trying to keep it friendly, so she smiled her biggest smile and said as sweetly as possibly, "T-G-I-F." The man smiled back at her and once again said, "S-H-I-T." The exasperated Kim finally decided to explain and said, "T-G-I-F" means Thank God, It's Friday. Get it, duuhhh?" The man answered, "'S-H-I-T' means "Sorry, Honey, It's Thursday... duuhhh."

A Surgeon was checking on his patient Kim Kardashian after an operation and began to like you would hold your boyfriends penis." That said, she takes the club and hits the ball. The Pro says, "That was a great shot... right down the runway. Now take the club out of your mouth, put it in your hands and we'll go for distance."

Kim, Kourtney and Khloe Kardashian get on the elevator of a Large Apartment Complex. Khloe looks down and sees a white spot on the carpet and says, "That looks like Sperm." Kourtney reaches down and rubs it around in her fingers and says, "That feels like Sperm." Kim reaches down rubs it in her fingers, tastes it, tastes it again and says, "It is Sperm, but it's not from anyone in this building."

Kourtney says, "Last night I made love with this guy and it was soooo good, I had two orgasms." Khloe says, "Oh yeah, last night I had sex with a guy and had four orgasms." Kim says, "That's nothing... last night was soooo for a kosher hot dog, would you ask if I'm Jewish, if I asked for a Taco, would you ask if I'm Mexican?" The Clerk says, "Well, No. Probably not." Kim angrily asks, "Then why ask if I'm Polish just because I asked for Polish Sausage?" The Clerk replies, "Because you're in Home Depot."

Kim Kardashian decides to try horseback riding for the first time. She mounts it and it starts to gallop. She begins to slip from the saddle and becoming fearful, she throws her arms around the horse's neck but slides down the side. Petrified, she tries to throw herself off but her foot gets stuck in the stirrup. She is at the horse's mercy as her head hits the ground. Kim is almost unconscious, when luckily the Walmart greeter rushes out and Unplugs the Horse.

Kim Kardashian goes for her first Golf lesson. The Pro says, "You've got to hold the club just

"You're not going to believe this but we did this puzzle in only four months." Then Kim says, "And on the box it says... from 3 to 5 years."

On a tour through an insane asylum, a couple pass a man in a padded cell holding a Large Doll crying. The guide says "That's a sad case. He was engaged to one of the Kardashian sisters, who left him the day before the wedding for another man." They continue walking and farther down the hallway in another padded cell, they see a man beating his head against a wall. The guide says, "And this Poor guy who keeps trying to kill himself... is the Other Man."

Kim Kardashian goes into a store and asks, "Where is the Polish sausage?" The Clerk says, "Are you Polish?" Kim replies, "Yes, I'm part Polish... but if I asked for Italian sausage would you ask if I'm Italian, If I asked

Kim Kardashian is showing off her new tattoo of a giant seashell on her upper inner thigh to her sisters. Kourtney asks, "Why would you get such a tattoo in that location?" Kim responded, "Because it's really cool. If you put your ear up against it, you can smell the Ocean."

Kim Kardashian's first husband arrived home unexpectedly and found her in bed with another man. Outraged, he screamed at her, "What the fuck is going on? Who is this man?" Kim replied, "That seems like a fair question." She then turned to the man in bed with her and said, "What is your name?"

Kim and Khloe are seated at a table with a Puzzle laid out when suddenly Kim places the final piece in and both of them begin screaming, "We did it. We did it." Their sister Kourtney walks in and asks, "What's all the commotion about?" Khloe excitedly says,

One afternoon, little ten-year-old Kim Kardashian ran up to her mom and said, "Mom, I just saw little Billy's wee wee next door." Kim's mom smiled and said, "Oh really?" Little Kim continued, "Yes... it's just like a peanut." Kim's mom smiled again and replied, "Oh yeah... that small, eh?" "No," said little Kim... "That salty."

When Kim Kardashian was 13 years old, she ran up to her Mom and said, "Mom, I know where babies come from." Kim's mom said, "Really, tell me." Little Kim answered, "Well, the mom and dad get naked. Then Daddy puts his thing in Mommy's mouth and he explodes and that's where babies come from." Kim's mom replied, "Oh honey, that's not where babies come from. That's where Jewelry comes from."

More Kardashian Jokes

It's the First day of school for little Kim Kardashian and the teacher asked the students to spell out their names. "S-U-E - S-M-I-T-H," said One, and the teacher replied, "Very good". "D-A-N - J-O-N-E-S," spelled out a 2nd student and the teacher said, "Excellent." The teacher then turned to Kim, who spelled, "K-I-M." The teacher replied, "No, I need your whole Name." "Oh," said Kim, and she spelled out... "V-A-G-I-N-A."

Returned Mail - MISS KIM KARDASHIAN: THANK YOU FOR YOUR RECENT ORDER FROM OUR SEX TOYS SHOP. YOU ASKED FOR THE LARGE RED VIBRATOR AS FEATURED ON OUR WALL DISPLAY. PLEASE SELECT ANOTHER ITEM BECAUSE THAT IS OUR FIRE EXTINGUISHER.

A Real estate man showing a new home to Kim Kardashian says, "This house has a living room, kitchen, 3 bedrooms and den." Kim replies, "And den what...?"

Kim to Doctor "Did I leave my Panties here at yesterday's check-up?" The Doctor says, "No." Kim says, "Dang, I must have left them at the Dentist."

A Kardashian Woman meets a basketball player at a party. She says, "You look just like my second husband." He asks her, "How many times have you been married?" She replies, "Once."

Kris Humphries said to Kim Kardashian on their honeymoon night, "Will I be the first?" Kim replied, "Even better... You'll be my hundred and first."

Kim brings her pet fish to a Veterinarian and says, "I think my goldfish has epilepsy." The Vet looks and it and says, "It seems calm to me." Kim replies, "I haven't taken it out of the bowl yet."

What's the difference between the Titanic and the Kardashian Women? Answer... Only 2,200 people went down on the Titanic.

What's the difference between the Kardashian Women and a Parrot? Answer... You can teach a Parrot to say "No."

What's the difference between an Italian Wife and a Kardashian Wife? An Italian Wife has Real Orgasms... and Fake Diamonds.

Kim Kardashian comes home and finds five guys sitting on her doorstep. She says to them, "Look, I've been working all day, and I'm really tired... so One of you has to go home."

Quickie Kardashian Jokes

What do the Kardashian Women put behind their ears to attract men? Answer... Their ankles.

How come the Kardashian Women never blink during foreplay? Because they don't have enough time.

How does a Volcano differ from the Kardashian Women? Answer... Volcanoes don't Fake eruptions.

THE KARDASHIAN SISTERS lost money when they designed a Fur Coat made from Chimpanzees because too many people complained that the Sleeves were too Long.

THE KARDASHIAN SISTERS' future plans include forming a group called "Divorce Anonymous." If a Celebrity gets an urge to Divorce, they send an Accountant to talk them out of it.

Kardashian Future Business Ideas

THE KARDASHIAN SISTERS plan on opening a new fast food take-out place in Beverly Hills called... "Kentucky Fried Caviar"

THE KARDASHIAN SISTERS have created a chocolate bar with "lettuce" in the center for women on a diet.

THE KARDASHIAN SISTERS have designed a wedding cake where on the top will be a miniature bride, groom and divorce lawyer.

"Virgins are rare... In a survey of 50,000 pregnant women... not one was found."

"The Two Things that cause the most problems in marriage... are Men and Women."

"If it weren't for Marriage... Husbands and Wives would have to Fight with Strangers."

"If you drink a glass of milk every day for a hundred years... you'll be a hundred years old."

"Always get married in the morning... because that way, if it doesn't work out... you won't spoil the whole day."

"Whether youre rich or poor... it's nice to have money."

"The trouble with Opera... is there's too much singing."

"People would be Healthier... if they didn't get sick so much."

"Money is just green stuff with pictures of dead people on it."

"If there's 3 things I can't stand... it's stupidity and ignorance."

"All I ask is a chance to prove that money can't make me happy."

"I never watch a movie unless I've seen it before... then I know it's good."

"A beautiful woman does not have to be great in bed... but an ugly woman does."

Misquotes by the Kardashian Women

"3 out of 4 divorces end in marriage."

"Its not the size, it's... no, it's the size..."

"Which wine goes best with more wine...?"

"Of all my relations... I still like sex the best."

"Is it me... or do buffalo wings taste like chicken?"

Kanye once showed up at Kim's house and found her sliding down the banister NUDE. She told him that she was warming up dinner.

Before having sex, Kim always asks Kanye to pour Coca Cola on his thing... because she heard that "Things" go better with Coke.

Kim went to the Doctor, who noticed she had "Wax" on her belly button. When he asked her why, Kim explained that Kanye likes to "Eat" by candlelight.

Kanye's sexual preference is "Rodeo Sex." He likes to mount Kim from behind, then say to her, "I fucked your sister last night, who was much better." Then he tries to hold on for 8 seconds.

Kanye thinks Kim is such a great lover... that he had seatbelts installed on their bed.

Kim and Kanye were recently in a traffic accident when Kanye was driving and Kim got her high heel stuck in the steering wheel.

Kanye knew Kim was truly in love with him when she was willing to have sex with him... right after she had her hair done.

One of the biggest fights Kim and Kanye have had was over her iPhone. Kanye wanted Kim to quit texting during sex.

Kim taught Kanye that the quickest way for him to turn her on was to "Lick" her belly button... from the inside.

On Kim and Kanye

When Kanye first saw Kim in a bar, he said, "Hey gorgeous, I don't like to waste time, so you wanna fuck or not?" Kim replied, "Normally I don't but you've talked me into it."

When Kanye and Kim first met, it was "Sex at first sight."

When Kim first looked into Kanye's eyes, she fell madly in love... when she saw her reflection.

Kim was once offered a small part in movie and was so insulted she laughed in the Producer's Balls.

Kim considers herself a "Quadrasexual"... which is... Someone who will do Anything with Anyone... for a "Quarter."

Kim once impressed her boyfriend by ordering an entire meal in French... which confused the waiter because it was a Chinese restaurant.

Kim once went to the Doctor and asked if he could remove her love handles. He said, "I can remove your love handles, but it might affect your hearing."

Kim's idea of a "Quiet" evening at home... is "Fucking" a Mime Troupe.

As a young girl, Kim had birth control pills in the shape of the Flintstones.

Kim admits when she was thirteen, she was a virgin but was not a fanatic about it.

Kim's mother stopped spanking her at 10 years old after she caught Kim reading an "S&M" magazine.

After her last Marriage, Kim tried to form a New Group: "Sex without partners."

Kim once almost got hurt when she tripped over her 7-inch heels... but luckily, her eylashes broke the fall.

Kim once burnt her tongue on the toaster... trying to make "French" Toast.

Kim got her first Dog from the Pound. She said if she couldn't have one naturally, she may as well adopt one.

Kim has beautiful Legs... and the right kind... One on each side.

Kim once took a birth control pill with some polluted water... and woke up stagnant.

Kim's all-time favorite Christmas Gift was a "Mistletoe Belt Buckle."

On Kim's Driver's License, it specifies that she "must wear Underwear."

Things You Might Not Know About Kim Kardashian

Kim's favorite word is... "Moist"

It's easy to know when Kim has an orgasm... because she always drops her nail file.

Kim saved a piece of her wedding cake for her divorce lawyer.

Kim's Butt

In a survey conducted, 9 out of 10 men said they thought Kim Kardashian had a nice butt. The 10th man preferred the other 9 men's butts.

Kim Kardashian's Ass is how the phrase... "The end justifies the means" got started?

If Kim was told to Haul Ass... she'd have to make at least two trips.

Kim always gets married for better or worse: Better for her, worse for him.

Kim Kardashian admits the reason she divorced Kris Humphries, who is half black, was finding out on their Honeymoon that it's the Top Half.

On Kim

Kim is a woman who thinks it's every Man for Herself.

Kim's idea of a threesome is her and the Chicago Bears.

Kim Kardashian has more talent in her little finger... than she has in her whole body.

Kim Kardashian doesn't marry for better or worse... but for more or less.

Kim to Khloe after their breakup: "Not only did he break my heart and ruin my life, but he spoiled my entire evening."

Khloe: "They say there's a difference between having sex being single and having sex commiting adultery."
Kim: "I don't know about that. I've tried 'em both and they seem the same to me."

Khloe: "I'm a vegetarian, which means I only eat vegetables."
Kim: "MMMmmm... Well, that must mean I'm a humanitarian."

What You Might Hear at a Kardashian Family Dinner

"I'm not getting my two-year-old daughter an agent for at least one more year. I want her to have a normal childhood."

Kim to Khloe: "Are you sexually active?"
Khloe: "No, I just lie there."

Kim to Khloe: "Last year I dated over fifty guys and haven't had sex with one of them."
Khloe: "Really... which one?"

Kardashians' Views on Politics

Politicians are saying they want to eliminate Poverty... which is ridiculous. That's all a lot of people have left.

We believe in the Death Penalty... How else are you going to stop people from changing lanes without using their turn signal?

Of course Mitt Romney has sex appeal... but it's all in a Cayman Island bank account.

Sometimes it's better to have loved and lost than to have loved and won.

If someone you Love walks out on you... always remember to shut the door.

Relationships are similar to the stock market... They're both easier to get into than out of.

When you resist temptation, you'll feel happiness... When you give in to it, you'll feel "Greater" happiness.

The Kardashians' Views on Philosophy

Life is like a Penis... it often gets HARD for No Reason.

Let them that don't want... have memories of not getting any.

Anything is possible... if you don't know what you're talking about.

Kardashian Views on SEX

Never have sex with anyone crazier than yourself.

Never look down on anyone... unless they're going down on you.

Never make Love on a Railroad Track... because a Train might "Come" before YOU do.

"Oral" Sex

THE KARDASHIAN WOMEN believe that Oral Sex... is the sincerest form of flattery.

THE KARDASHIAN WOMEN believe that the worst thing about Oral Sex... is the View.

THE KARDASHIAN WOMEN believe that Oral sex is great but can be very lonely because while you're doing it, you have no one to talk to.

THE KARDASHIAN WOMEN believe that Girls eventually Lose their Virginity... but they still get to keep the Box it came in.

THE KARDASHIAN WOMEN believe that good girls might get to go to heaven... but bad girls get to go everywhere.

THE KARDASHIAN WOMEN believe that If God didn't want us to play with oursleves... He wouldn't have made our hands reach that far.

THE KARDASHIAN WOMEN believe that Sex is usually the first thing on a man's mind. The second, third and fourth are how, where and when.

THE KARDASHIAN WOMEN believe that Sex is a lot like Chess... There's a lot of moves... but the ending is always the same.

On Sex

THE KARDASHIAN WOMEN have morals. They are always the last ones to get naked at an Orgy.

THE KARDASHIAN WOMEN rarely have sex in the morning, because they never know who they might meet in the afternoon.

THE KARDASHIAN WOMEN Fake Orgasms... because Men Fake Foreplay.

Nowadays, The Kardashians take Vitamin Pills to get into shape... and birth control Pills to stay that way.

On Dieting

The Kardashians believe that Men should never Underestimate a Woman... unless they're talking about her Age or her Weight.

According to the Kardashians, their dream is not to find the perfect guy... but to eat whatever they want without getting fat.

The Kardashians have hired a food scientist to figure out why a 2-pound box of candy can make a woman gain 10 pounds?

Top 5 Signs a Kardashian Marriage might not last

1) If after the Minister says "Do you take this man to honor, love and obey?" she responds, "Whatever!!!"

2) If she has Towels made marked... "HERS and NEXT"

3) If her Wedding Gown is "Wash 'n' Wear."

4) If after the wedding, everyone throws Minute Rice.

5) If both of her sisters move in.

The Honeymoon

Kim Kardashian reports that after her next marriage, Her Honeymoon will be filmed and later released as a Workout Video.

The Kardashians believe that you should always enjoy your Honeymoon. They only happen every 2 or 3 years.

Something you'll never hear... A Kardashian saying "ouch" on her Honeymoon.

To a Kardashian... the Real Secret to a Successful Marriage is... finding someone you love to "Argue" with.

To a Kardashian... marriage is like Playing Cards. In the beginning all you need is two hearts and a diamond. By the end you wish you had a fucking club and a spade.

Usually, a Kardashian marriage proposal goes like this: "How'd you like to do this every night?"

To a Kardashian... Marriage is a wonderful way to spend a weekend.

To a Kardashian... a Marriage license is very important. Without one, you can't get a divorce.

To a Kardashian... June is the month for weddings... the other eleven are for divorces.

To a Kardashian... While waiting for the right man to come along... it's okay to get married in the meantime.

To a Kardashian... Marriage is a private affair and what goes on in it should be kept between the 5 to 20 people involved.

Kardashian Views on Marriage

To a Kardashian... Marriage is For Richer... or Forget it.

To a Kardashian... You can live happily and get married forever after.

To a Kardashian... Marriage always works best... as a last resort.

To a Kardashian... Marriage is a wonderful rest stop... between relationships.

When a Kardashian has a wedding... they're so happy, they can hardly wait for the next one.

A Kardashian wedding... is where the wedding cake... outlasts the wedding.

At a Kardashian wedding, they believe it's for better or for worse... but not for long.

Most women save their wedding dresses for their daughters. The Kardashians save them for their next wedding.

Some people Marry for Love, Some people Marry for Money... but the Kardahsians Marry for a Short Time.

On Weddings

Telling a Kardashian what she should know on their wedding night is sort of like giving a fish a bath.

When the Kardashian Girls think of marriage, they have to consider one thing: Is this the man I want my kids to spend weekends with?

The reason you never see a Kardashian Woman cry at weddings is because they all know it's so easy to get a divorce.

THE KARDASHIAN WOMEN believe that there are many ways to say, "I Love You"... but "FUCKING"... is still the best.

THE KARDASHIAN WOMEN believe there are 10 Things girls should not say the first time they see a New Boyfriend's Penis:

1) "I've smoked fatter joints than that."
2) "Ahhhh, it's so cute."
3) "You got to be kidding."
4) "Wow, and your feet are so big."
5) "This explains your car."
6) "Maybe if we water it, it'll grow."
7) "Are you cold?"
8) "Do you mind if I get real drunk first?"
9) "What is that? I'll get the tweezers and get rid of it."
10) "Why don't we just cuddle?"

THE KARDASHIAN WOMEN believe that "Charisma"... is that indescribable something... that women with "Big Tits and Big Asses" have.

THE KARDASHIAN WOMEN believe that if your palm itches... you're going to get something. If your groin itches... you've already got something.

THE KARDASHIAN WOMEN believe that whoever said Money can't buy Happiness, Love or Respect... is obviously a terrible shopper.

THE KARDASHIAN WOMEN believe that a real Gentleman is someone who offers to sleep in the "Wet" spot.

THE KARDASHIAN WOMEN believe that real beauty is on the inside... at least that's what all the "Ugly" women say.

THE KARDASHIAN WOMEN believe that nothing is more annoying than NOT being invited to a party you wouldn't have gone to anyway.

THE KARDASHIAN WOMEN believe that it doesn't matter if a girl loses their virginity... She still gets to keep the "Box" it came in.

THE KARDASHIAN WOMEN believe that for most women, Life is an endless struggle, full of frustration and challenges... until they find a Hair Stylist they like.

THE KARDASHIAN WOMEN believe that if at first you don't succeed... try using foreplay.

THE KARDASHIAN WOMEN believe that if at first you don't succeed... try, try again... she expects you to.

THE KARDASHIAN WOMEN believe that if at first you don't succeed... try again when nobody is watching.

THE KARDASHIAN WOMEN believe that it's not the thought that counts, but the gift behind it.

THE KARDASHIAN WOMEN believe that you should Never Look Down on Anyone... Unless They're Going Down on You.

THE KARDASHIAN WOMEN believe that Time may be a Great Healer..... but Plastic Surgery is quicker.

THE KARDASHIAN WOMEN believe that 29 is a nice age for a woman... especially if she's in her thirties.

THE KARDASHIAN WOMEN believe that as Bad Habits go... Adultery beats Nail-biting.

THE KARDASHIAN WOMEN believe that women are great housekeepers... especially after their divorce.

THE KARDASHIAN WOMEN believe that "One good turn"... gets most of the covers...

THE KARDASHIAN WOMEN believe that you should start each day out with a Bang.

THE KARDASHIAN WOMEN believe that if you can get a man by the "Balls"... his heart and mind will soon follow.

THE KARDASHIAN WOMEN believe a bird in the hand... is not as much fun... as a hand in the bush.

THE KARDASHIAN WOMEN believe that when in Rome... sleep with all the Romans.

THE KARDASHIAN WOMEN believe that "Panties" may not be the best thing in life... but they're right "next" to it.

What the Kardashians Believe

THE KARDASHIAN WOMEN believe that GOD gave them "Nipples" to make "Suckers" out of Men.

THE KARDASHIAN WOMEN believe that it's better to be looked over... than to be overlooked.

THE KARDASHIAN WOMEN believe that Love means never having to say... "Next."

When a Kardashian Woman meets a man, their eyes meet, then their lips meet, then their hearts meet, then their bodies meet, then their souls meet... then their Lawyers meet.

One Kardashian Woman talking by herself is a Monologue. All three Kardashian Women talking is a Cat-alogue.

The Kardashian Women get boob jobs, wear wigs, false eyelashes and fake fingernails... And then say they're looking for a "REAL" MAN.

When a Kardashian Woman is asked by a guy if he's the first she's ever had sex with... She usually replies, "Do you want my stock answer...??"

If one of the Kardashian Women says she loves you from the bottom of her heart, that most likely means there's lots of room at the top for others.

The Kardashian Women love having sex under the Stars. (Basketball Stars)

The Kardashian Women are always looking for a secure, meaningful, lasting... one-night stand.

The Kardashian Women don't mind telling men that they love them.... they just don't like to write it.

The Kardashian Women can do "without" everything in this world... except self indulgence.

Some women count on their fingers... The Kardashian Women count on their Legs, Tits and Asses.

The Kardashian Women

The Kardashian Women always try to put up a Good Front.

The Kardashian Women like the simple things in life: "MEN."

The Kardashian Women always think twice... before saying "Nothing"...

The Kardashian Women always prefer a Man who's either Single or Married.

KRIS KARDASHIAN is currently writing a novel about her daughter Kim. It's fiction and called *I was a Teenage Virgin*.

KRIS KARDASHIAN taught her daughters that if you hear no evil, see no evil and speak no evil... you'll never be part of a reality show.

When the Kardashian girls were teenagers, KRIS KARDASHIAN always reminded them that... Eve "slept" with the FIRST man that she met.

When the Kardashian girls were kids, KRIS KARDASHIAN always told them that when they grew up, they could be anything they wanted to be... so they became sex addicts.

When the Kardashian girls were small kids, KRIS KARDASHIAN would pay $1,500 for a graduation dress for them. She said, "It's only once that a girl goes from kindergarten to first grade."

Mom Kardashian

When the Kardashian girls were little, their favorite bedtime story that KRIS KARDASHIAN would tell them was... "Once upon a time there were Three Bears. A mama bear, a papa bear and a baby bear by a previous marriage."

Kris Kardashian was trying to have her fidgety teenage daughters prepare for a photo session and told them, "Be still girls, the photographer wants to focus." Young Kim replied, "All of us."

The KARDASHIANS May not be all there... but there's enough there to make it worthwhile.

When you look at the KARDASHIANS, you realize it costs a fortune... to look cheap.

For the Kardashians, a silver anniversary is being married twenty-five times.

Now Let's Get Started

Behind every Kardashian Woman... is a guy... staring at her ass.

The KARDASHIANS are proof that in hollywood, Blood is thicker than talent.

They say you are what you eat... which explains why the KARDASHIANS all look so "Cocky"

Introduction

When Einstein died and arrived in heaven, St. Peter wouldn't let him in until he proved his identity. Einstein scribbled out some of his equations, and was admitted into paradise. When Picasso died, St. Peter asked, "How do I know you're Picasso?" Picasso sketched out a few of his masterpieces, St. Peter was convinced and let him in. When Kim Kardashian died, she went to heaven and St. Peter asked, "How can you prove you're Kim Kardashian?" Kim replied, "I don't know." St. Peter said, "Albert Einstein showed me his equations and Picasso drew his famous pictures. How can you prove you're Kim Kardashian?" Kim said, "Who are Albert Einstein and Picasso?" St. Peter said, "Okay Kim, it's you. C'mon on in."

The JOKE Book

for people who think the KARDASHIANS are a joke

The Joke Book for People Who Think The Kardashians are a Joke
© 2013 The Unknown Comic. All rights reserved.

No part of this book may be reproduced in any form or by any means, electronic, mechanical, digital, photocopying or recording, except for the inclusion in a review, without permission in writing from the publisher.

Published in the USA by:
BearManor Media
PO Box 1129
Duncan, OK 73534-1129
www.BearManorMedia.com

ISBN-10: 1593932588
ISBN-13: 1-59393-258-8

Cover design and layout by Allan T. Duffin.

Printed in the United States of America

The JOKE Book

for people who think the KARDASHIANS are a joke

by THE UNKNOWN COMIC

BearManor Media

Albany, Georgia

www.ingramcontent.com/pod-product-compliance
Lightning Source LLC
Chambersburg PA
CBHW051106160426
43193CB00010B/1331